Grief

Through Different Eyes

a memoir

Wendyanne Pakulsky

©2022 by Wendyanne Pakulsky

All rights reserved. No part of this book may be reproduced, distributed, or transmitted in any form or by any means, including photocopying, recording, or other electronic or mechanical methods, without the prior written permission of the publisher, except in the case of brief quotations embodied in critical articles, reviews, and certain other noncommercial uses permitted by copyright law.

This story is inspired by true events, which are recounted to the best of the author's recollection.

ISBN: 978-0-6456194-0-9

*To my beautiful cousin,
soul sister, and
lifelong earth angel,
Alison de Vink.*

*You have always walked with
me through this journey, and
your unconditional love,
strength, and support have
never faltered—and are still as
strong as ever.*

I love you, Alison.

*Yesterday, I cried.
I cried because I hurt.
I cried because I was hurt.
I cried because hurt has
no place to go
except deeper into the pain
that caused it in the first place,
and when it gets there,
the hurt wakes you up.
I cried because it was too late.
I cried because it was time.
In the midst of my crying,
I felt my freedom coming.*

— Iyanla Vanzant

Contents

Foreword 7

Introduction 11

The Sunset 19

The Beginning and the End 51

A Fresh Start 99

Forgiveness Through Different Eyes ... 103

Epilogue 117

Acknowledgements 123

About the Author 133

Foreword

By Alison de Vink

GRIEF THROUGH DIFFERENT EYES is the courageous testament of one woman's struggle to find herself and bring meaning into her life after enduring the difficulties of growing up under the control of an abusive father—a man quick to anger and lash out, a man lacking in empathy or understanding of the impact he had on how she grew up to view both herself and her place in the world.

Brutally honest and raw, the narrative captivates the reader with the author's highly vulnerable and emotionally delicate account of how she survives childhood, enters adulthood, and begins the arduous journey of unpacking, processing, and putting into perspective her life experiences, which ultimately leads her to a place of healing and self-love.

Over the course of my own life, I've had the honour and the privilege, as well as the heartache and despair, of witnessing the author—my dear and precious soul-sister, friend, and cousin—as she's endured, developed, and grown. I've seen the deeply painful low points she's braved as well as the incredible resilience she's demonstrated throughout the process of reclaiming her life.

Foreword

I've also witnessed this beautiful woman's heart-wrenching decision to finally sever ties with her father after multiple attempts to develop a more amicable and sustainable relationship with him—a decision made out of sheer desperation and finally acceptance that with some people, it's best to leave them in the past and go on alone without them. This decision marked the true beginning of her finding the courage to face head-on the trauma she'd experienced growing up and into her early adulthood.

While reading and following this heroic woman's story, one can't help but be struck by the miraculous transformation that takes place over the course of many years as she not only finds her strength, peace, and voice but also allows her true essence to shine brightly, illuminating the pathway in life for those whom she holds dear.

As a lucky recipient of her unconditional love, acceptance, wisdom, and commitment to my own well-being, I am truly blessed.

So here's to you, my darling Wendyanne, for putting pen to paper and allowing us to share in your story. You, my sweet girl, never cease to amaze and inspire those who truly know you as I do. Your kindness and ability to relate to even the youngest of children is certainly a reflection of what it is that truly fills your heart.

Introduction

SHORTLY AFTER MY FATHER DIED, my therapist gave me a book about grief. I went home and read the whole thing, cover to cover. And I resonated with absolutely none of it.

So I went to a bookstore and looked through other books on grieving. Again, I didn't connect with the experiences these authors described. I also read books that were given to me by other well-meaning people who wanted to help me through the grieving process. But I just couldn't relate to anything in these books. Not one thing.

It seemed like they all described how society expects the grieving process to unfold—the five stages, the intense pain, the longing to have the person alive and well and in your life again. I know that for many people, this is exactly how grief feels.

But what if your experience of grief is different?

What if you don't go through the typical stages? What if you don't feel what others feel? What if you don't grieve the way society expects you to? Or what if you don't grieve at all? Does that mean there's something wrong with you? That you're heartless? That you're not "normal"?

And what if the person you lost was a parent? Does that make a difference?

Introduction

We all know how you're "supposed" to feel when you lose a parent with whom you had a close, loving relationship. But how do you grieve for them if your relationship was far from ideal? How do you grieve for a parent who mistreated you, disrespected you, abused you, neglected you, or left you? How do you grieve for a person when your relationship with them already died years earlier, when you've already grieved while they were still alive?

This was my experience. But as I was going through it, no one seemed to be talking about anything like it—not the books I read, not the people I talked to, and certainly not the online grief-support groups I went to, where I was called heartless, horrible…and far worse.

I knew I wasn't heartless, though. I was—and still am—an incredibly sensitive, loving woman. My experience was simply different from the norm.

Years before my father died, our relationship died. After many years of emotional and physical abuse—and more years of unsuccessfully attempting to build a healthy relationship—I finally severed ties with him. And so I grieved him while he was still alive. By the time he passed, I had already gone through my own stages of grief. I had already hit rock bottom and felt despair, deflation, disappointment, and sheer exhaustion from trying to carry what was never mine to carry—from trying to break the chains that had held me down for years, from trying to find my true voice and my true self, from trying to truly live.

Fortunately, after I told my therapist about my experience—and how I couldn't relate to the book she'd given me—she was very understanding. With her help, the compassion of a few close friends, and the grace of God, I have been able to emerge from these difficult experiences stronger than ever. But I can tell you that if I had found a book like this—a

Introduction

book that described experiences similar to my own—it would have helped me tremendously. It would have let me know that there was nothing wrong with me and that I wasn't alone.

And that's why I'm writing this book now—to let you know that if your grieving experience is different from others', there's nothing wrong with you. If you've had a complicated relationship with your deceased parent—or if you've had a difficult time grieving for a parent who was absent, neglectful, or abusive—you're not alone. And if you're ready to emerge from a dark time, step into your light, and claim your power, there is hope.

I've gone through it, and I can tell you that it is possible to find joy, light, and life on the other side of these painful experiences. And yes, they were very painful for me—so painful that I've been reluctant to write about them or share them with others. I didn't want to revisit such dark times and harrowing experiences.

And I didn't want to face any more hateful backlash. It felt easier to keep it all tucked away within me, out of sight from the world.

But as the years went by, I began to see that, as Anaïs Nin wrote, "the risk to remain tight in a bud was more painful than the risk it took to blossom." So, with my therapist's encouragement and God's help, I embarked on a journey of survival, strength, and, ultimately, serenity. I learned to unbecome everything I am not and to grow towards everything I am meant to be. I chose what nourished my soul. I blossomed. I set myself free.

Through my journey, I've learned that even if you have a very different version of grief than what society expects, you can still experience your own unique form of acceptance, serenity, and grace. So, as painful as it is at times, that's why I'm choosing to share my story now. I know that it won't resonate with everyone, but I hope it can open

Introduction

some people's eyes and hearts to other forms of grief. And I hope it can help others who have gone through similar experiences. Most of all, I hope it can help you.

Even if the details of your experiences are quite different from mine, I hope you'll find some comfort in knowing that there's not just one "right" (or "wrong") way to grieve. You can see grief through different eyes. And you can find life on the other side of grief. You can blossom.

All my love,
Wendyanne

The Sunset

18 December 2018

WHAT A BEAUTIFUL YEAR IT HAD BEEN.

It was my last day of another year of teaching kindergarten in Victoria, Australia, and I was enjoying the children's Christmas concert. As they were singing and dancing, they looked like petals blowing blissfully in a spring breeze. I couldn't help but smile and connect with their joy.

I always love working with children. Part of my soul rejoices in their innocence, which reawakens a long-forgotten piece of my own spirit. And on this day, I savoured that delight more than ever.

After the concert, as I hugged the children goodbye and wished them well for their next level of education, my soul rejoiced once again.

A beautiful ending to a beautiful year.

As I drove home, I felt bittersweet echoes of the year-end concert still stirring within me, but I was also looking forward to a relaxing six-week break. I turned up the music in my car and noticed that the sunset was extraordinarily beautiful that night, radiating a peaceful energy that told me that everything was good in the world.

The Sunset

I walked through my front door, kicked off my shoes, and heard a text message go off on my phone. I thought I would read it later that night or possibly even tomorrow. First, I took a long, hot shower and reflected on the day.

I felt a little sad seeing the children leave, as I did at the end of each year. The bonds I formed with them throughout the year were very real. Yet I knew that moving on was part of their growth, and I wondered what exciting adventures lay in front of them. I hoped that no matter what happened in their lives, they would carry beautiful memories of sunshine in their own hearts from their kindergarten year.

I got out of the shower, made a cup of English tea, and sat down on the sofa. Preparing to enjoy a quiet evening home alone, I decided to turn off my phone. But first I checked the unread text message. It was from my sister: "Dad had a massive brain haemorrhage early this morning and he is in hospital."

I read it a couple of times before I texted back. I simply wrote, "Thank you for letting me know." And I felt nothing—certainly not the shock most people would expect to feel if they had gotten such news.

I quietly drank my English tea, turned off my phone, went to bed, and fell straight off to sleep.

19 December

The next day, my reaction to the news was the same: I still felt nothing.

I was aware, however, that things would likely be changing in the coming days (or even hours). My six-week holiday, which I'd planned to spend relaxing, suddenly looked like it would be quite different from how I'd imagined. But I wanted to hold on to the peace and joy I'd felt yesterday, even if only for a little bit longer. So I spent the day alone in my garden. I didn't want people around me. I wanted to withdraw from the world, as I had done so many times before.

I had learned to withdraw at a very early age, and I still had no problem doing this. It was a survival skill, a coping mechanism that I had perfected. I knew exactly how to enter this place deep within myself, and I could do it very quickly—within seconds—a learned behaviour that I knew I would want to unlearn someday when I no longer wanted or needed to be in this place, someday when I felt safe and supported by the people in my life. To get to this place, I knew I would need to let go of what no longer served me on a healthy mental, physical, and spiritual level. But for now, here I was once again.

That afternoon, my sister texted me again, telling me my father had been taken into palliative care. She didn't elaborate, and I didn't ask for more details. I simply replied, "Thank you for letting me know." I knew that my sister was with him, along with one of my brothers and my father's partner and family, so he wouldn't be alone when the end came, which I assumed would be soon.

I prayed that the passing would be quick and that he wouldn't suffer. But I knew I would not be making the journey to see him. I had already said goodbye to him in the letter I'd written in a coffee shop seven years earlier.

20 December

The next morning, my sister texted me to say that my father was still alive but it wouldn't be long.

As I processed this information, I sensed that I was about to enter a stage of my life that to others can be absolutely devastating, yet I still felt nothing. I worried about my lack of reaction. Was this normal? Was I in shock? Why was I not feeling what society says I should be feeling at a time like this? After all, I'm not a heartless woman, but the feelings of grief simply were not there.

I had never lost a parent before, so I didn't know how I would react. Maybe after he passed, the feelings would hit me in the gut. But at this point, I wasn't sure what I was supposed to be feeling or even what outcome would be best. So I offered up a prayer and gently handed it over to God.

However, I did know that whatever happened with my father, I would be navigating the experience with almost no support from my family. My sister and I were very distant from each other at this point—not through anything we had done; life had simply divided us. I was grateful she had let me know about Dad, but I didn't expect anything beyond that—certainly not emotional comfort or understanding. I felt even more distant from my second-eldest brother, who'd had very different experiences with my father and therefore couldn't relate to what I'd gone through or how I was feeling (or not feeling) now. I was closer to my eldest brother; however, he lived in Perth—on the other side of the country—which made it difficult to maintain our close connection. And my mother had separated from my father thirty-seven years earlier, and she was uncomfortable talking about him.

If I needed to, I could always lean into my cousin Alison and also my therapist, both of whom had helped me through my healing journey. Neither had ever faltered in holding my hand as I walked through the dark into the light.

For the most part, however, I knew that I'd be going through this alone. So, no matter what anyone else thought—or what support or understanding they did or didn't offer—I knew I had to stay true to myself.

The Sunset

Later that day, I finally felt something about my father—a pang of guilt that I hadn't gone to see him. Part of me wondered if I should jump right into my car and drive to the hospital, but I knew that if I did, I'd be extremely angry at myself. After all, I'd done so much hard inner healing to reach a place of peace within my spirit, and I didn't want to risk that for anything ever again, particularly not for a man who had treated me with such cruelty and disdain, a man who had physically and emotionally abused me, a man who'd had no respect for me as a child, a teenager, a mum, or the woman I'd grown into. Still, I sensed the old patterns re-emerging—the little girl in me who always wanted to make it right for him. But I couldn't, and this time I wasn't even going to try. It was time to let that go.

My father was dying now, but our relationship had died a long time ago. What I was feeling now wasn't about him; it was about how I was going to emotionally support myself through this experience. I needed to show up for myself. It was time. It was more than time. And I was absolutely strong enough to do it. I had done enough inner work, and now I had to fully trust my decision and my spirit.

I had supported myself through hard times before, and I knew I would do it once again. And I would do it well. The love I was feeling for myself at this point took priority over anything else. It was extremely gentle and extremely strong. And I knew it would get me through this.

21 December

I woke up and put the kettle on. With Christmas only four days away, I still had some shopping to finish. But even as my mind was preoccupied with holiday preparations, I

The Sunset

knew this was going to be the day my father died.

On one level, I felt very calm. (Along with my survival technique of withdrawing, I have a wonderful way of pulling myself into a state of calm when I need to.) But I didn't know what to expect from the day. Because I was distanced from my family, I had no idea how to navigate this situation. I was just winging it.

I went out for lunch with a friend and waited to see how the day would unfold.

I felt prepared for my father's passing, although I had no idea how that was going to look. But I was still surprised by my lack of sadness. Instead, I felt increasingly uneasy about not feeling what society considered "normal"—not grieving in the "acceptable" way. I started to question myself: Was I regretting that at this point it was too late to drive into the city to say goodbye to my father? Could I have done anything to make it better or help him pass over? Was there something wrong with me because I felt no desire to go see him one last time?

But then I thought, why the fuck should I have to negotiate how I feel about my father's death? Who does that? Why should I have to compromise my boundaries or negotiate my strength?

When I looked to my spirit for guidance, it told me, loud and clear, "Wendyanne, you have done everything in your lifetime to build a relationship with this narcissistic, abusive man, and all he ever did was criticise, be angry and cruel, and never support anything you did."

I knew full well that my father was leaving this earth, and I was ready. But would I regret not going to see him one last time? I looked into my heart for guidance, and the answer was—and still is—*no!*

I had already done all I could. Now I was handing it over to God. It was time for me to keep leaning into my spirit and stay there until I was ready to move from that place within. I had no idea how long that would be, but it didn't matter. I just knew that, for now, this is where I needed to be.

Yes, I realised that when faced with a parent's imminent death, most people are absolutely gutted, like their world is going up in flames. But if anything, I felt like I was walking *out* of the flames—and my god, did it feel good!

When I returned from my outing, I cooked dinner for my daughter Sophia, and we wrapped Christmas presents. Then I had a shower and watched a movie. By 10 p.m., I still hadn't heard from my sister, and I didn't ring her. I knew she would contact me when she needed to.

At 10:30 I turned off my phone, went to bed, and fell straight off to sleep.

22 December

I woke at 2:30 a.m. and turned on my phone, and there it was: the text from my sister saying that Dad had just passed away. The text was sent to me at 11:36 the previous evening, only an hour after I had gone to bed. I turned my phone off again, rolled over, and went straight back to sleep.

I got up the next morning at 6:40 and put the kettle on. I was looking out the window at the sunrise, waiting for the kettle to boil, when Sophia walked into the kitchen. She said, "Are you okay, Mum?" I looked at her and said that my father had passed away last night. She hugged me, and I had a small cry. And then we shared a cup of tea.

I knew I wouldn't have any siblings around me on this day, which was perfectly fine with me. I was prepared to have a Wendyanne day. I did call my cousin Alison to tell her the news. Alison and I have an extremely beautiful connection, and I am so grateful that we've always shared a bond of unconditional love. As little girls, she and I were connected at the hip, and our emotional connection has only grown throughout our lives. There's nothing she doesn't know about me. I trust her completely and love her dearly.

Alison's mother, my father's sister, had passed away two years prior to my father, also of a brain haemorrhage, so I figured that if anyone could understand what I was going through, it would be her.

As I'd hoped, she did offer her love, compassion, and understanding, without any judgement about what I was (or wasn't) feeling—exactly what I needed.

After talking with Alison, I went off to a coffee shop just to watch the world go by. I had no idea how I was supposed to navigate this, I really didn't. All I knew was how calm I felt.

When my latte arrived at the table, I sat there, slowly stirring the sugar into it, feeling a calmness like I had never felt before. Maybe that was just shock, but it certainly didn't feel like shock. It felt like serenity.

I was surrounded by people in the coffee shop coming and going, and everything felt like it was in slow motion. There was Christmas music playing, and I felt like a hundred angels were dancing around me, supporting me in love and light.

I was as peaceful as peaceful gets.

For the first time in my life, I didn't have to worry about running into him. The fight was over. And I was not going to let go of this feeling of peacefulness—not for anyone.

There was no place I had to be. So for the next three hours I just sat in this coffee shop where seven years prior I had written the most profound letter—a letter that no daughter should ever have had to write to her father. I had finally come home to myself, and it was such a beautiful place to be.

23 December

Today I just wanted to be near the water, which is where my soul feels most peaceful. I'm always happy around lakes, rivers, the ocean, or anywhere that has sand that I can sink my toes into. So my daughter, grandbabies, and I took the boat out with some friends. We left very early, stopping to have breakfast before getting on the boat.

The day was exactly what I needed. The lake was so calm, and the sky was beautiful. So much of this day was about hugging my grandbabies and watching their faces when we talked about finding Nemo in the water.

And I was happy.

I was happy to be on the water and happy to be with loved ones, but it was deeper than that. Being on the boat was so invigorating, and the water felt so expansive, stretching for miles all around us. I felt alive. I felt peaceful. I felt free.

24 December

Christmas Day was almost here, and still I had only cried once—when I hugged my daughter the morning just after my father had passed away.

I was having English tea in my garden when a text went off on my phone. It was my sister saying, "If you want to put a piece in the paper it has to be in by 10 o'clock this morning."

I just replied, "Thanks."

As heartless as my reply may have seemed, it was all I wanted to say. I chose not to put an obituary in the paper, and the day went on as planned.

I finished wrapping presents and cooked for the next day, as we were having Christmas at my daughter's home. Throughout it all, I stayed focused on the day I would be having with my grandbabies, my daughters, and my mum.

25 December

I woke up on Christmas morning and, more than at any other time in my life, I just wanted to spend the day alone.

I knew the strength I would have to find just to get through another day of my father's death going unacknowledged. It's not that I was in deep grief and wanted sympathy, but I also didn't want the topic to be taboo. I don't know what was harder: the fact that no family had mentioned my father's passing or the fact that I felt I couldn't bring it up. In either case, I just wanted to be a million miles from everyone. Instead, I got up and prepared to go to my daughter's house for a Christmas celebration.

Once I got there, I felt even more unsettled. I played with my grandbabies and talked to my mum and both of my daughters and their partners, but no one mentioned the death. My sister and brothers weren't there, and no one else in my family seemed to be thinking about it at all—or, if they were, they certainly didn't let on.

Despite my festive façade, I was really struggling at this point. Throughout the day, it hit me that none of this seemed fair—none of it—and I had no idea how I was supposed to handle it and I was really fucking angry with God and I didn't want anyone near me. But on the outside, I acted as if everything were fine.

When I came home from my daughter's that evening, my sister texted me that Dad's funeral would be on 28 December at 2 p.m. She also told me the church where it would be held. What was I supposed to do with this information? What difference did it make to me? After all, I knew I wouldn't be going. I'd have no place there where my spirit would feel comfortable, and I didn't want any part of it.

I didn't feel close enough to my sister at that point to mention any of this. And I certainly wasn't going to discuss it with my second eldest brother. Even though he lived nearby and is the sibling who's closest to me in terms of age, I'd never been able to relate to him, and now we were estranged from each other. He had always been very close to my father, and now he'd be organising the funeral and certainly wouldn't understand my need to stay away.

My eldest brother lived far away, but I did get to talk to him on the phone. He didn't want to talk about our father's passing, though. I wished we were together so that I could give him a hug, but I just wished him a Merry Christmas and left it at that.

I felt like an only child, left alone to fend for herself.

Had that letter I'd written to my father given away all my rights as a daughter? Was this the price for finally saying that I matter more than his narcissistic abuse? After a lifetime of mistreatment, I'd finally had enough. In that letter, I had been very clear that my father was not to contact me ever again and that, if he did, I would have no choice but to have an intervention taken out on him. I'd had enough.

I needed to break free, to protect myself on all levels, so I had set clear, strong boundaries in that letter—boundaries that I continued to honour and strengthen for the remainder of his life. But what did those boundaries mean now that he was gone?

26 December

Once Christmas was over, I felt flat. I stayed at home and slept most of the day. I did get out in the garden in the morning, but the afternoon was mostly spent sleeping.

27 December

At this point I hadn't heard anything more from my sister, but I figured she was busy getting things ready for the funeral. I knew there was a viewing today, although I wasn't invited. It didn't really matter, though, since I wouldn't have gone anyway.

I did speak to my cousin Alison again. As the funeral was the next day, I asked her, "Do I go to the funeral or not?" I had already made up my mind that I wouldn't be there, but I still wanted her perspective on it.

She replied, "My darling Wendyanne, you'll be damned if you don't and damned if you do, so you need to do what's right for you."

Her answer was a breath of fresh air. I finally had someone from my family really acknowledge my situation, provide clarity, and reassure me about my decision. And instead of trying to impose society's expectations on me, she honoured the decision that I had already made completely out of love and light for myself. Once again, I felt blessed to have Ally in my life—to receive her unconditional love and respect.

28 December

I woke up early on the morning of my father's funeral, and I felt absolutely nothing. I could hardly believe it, but once again that was my truth. Today was my father's funeral, and I felt nothing!

The funeral would be at 2 p.m., and I wanted to be as far away from it as possible. So I decided to go to the beach with a friend. As I've mentioned, I always feel very peaceful at the beach. It has never failed to calm my spirit. And today of all days, that's exactly what I needed.

I couldn't get out of the house soon enough. I left at 10 a.m., picked up my friend, and went out for lunch near the water. As I ate, I began looking at the time and felt numb. Should I have been in this place, miles away from where my father was about to be laid to rest? I didn't know, but I felt like a higher calling had drawn me to the ocean that day.

After lunch, we spent the afternoon by the water. As I'd hoped, it was a calm day—exactly what my soul needed. As I sat gazing out at the ocean, I wondered once again: was I in the right place or not? But this time I knew the answer: yes, I absolutely was.

Sometimes going against the grain is the only way to honour yourself, and my decision today was not about anyone else in my family. It was a very sacred contract between God and myself.

I was certain that not going to my father's funeral felt like the right decision for me. While driving home, however, I was struck by an urge to go to my father's grave. Where had this feeling come from? Well, I certainly hadn't wanted to go to his funeral, but I did want to go to his grave after the burial—by myself, after everyone else had gone.

So, at 6 p.m. I dropped my friend off and drove up to the cemetery. It was a very old cemetery overlooking a huge lake. When I arrived, the sun was setting, and the glow on the lake was beautiful.

I slowly got out of my car and stood at the cemetery gate before I opened it. I looked around, and there it was—to the right, two rows down—my father's grave, freshly covered up. I knew that nobody in my family would be at the cemetery at that time, which is why I chose to go then. It was just my father and me.

I walked over to the grave and just stared at it, feeling nothing, not shedding one single tear. I took in the scene around me, and the silence felt beautiful. I looked backed at the grave, and all I could say was, "I wish you well." Then I walked away.

I had been there for a total of two minutes.

The Sunset

I went to get into my car, but before I got in, I looked back at the grave one more time, and I felt a huge lightness—almost like the energy that had been protecting me that day was once again with me—and I heard a whisper in my ear: "His game is now over."

I got into my car and drove off with my music playing, and I felt like my life was just beginning.

I spent the next four hours with Alison at her home just talking, feeling as light as a feather. Once again, her unconditional love made my whole day worthwhile.

Ally has always had a way of talking me through things that I can't see clearly for myself. She just comes along like an angel and explains it to me in a way that my soul understands. She certainly did that on this night when I needed her understanding more than ever. She told me that my aura was beautiful—calm and peaceful—and I could feel every single bit of that.

29 December

The day after my father's funeral, I felt flat and in protective mode. I had no idea what would be coming at me today, but I wasn't expecting any family conversation. This was fine with me, as I didn't want anyone near me today. One hundred kilometres away still would have been too close for me.

I kept my phone off all day and spent most of the day in my garden. I felt lucky to be home on my own. This is exactly where I wanted to be.

As my mind played over the end of my father's life, I thought, how the fuck did things go so, so wrong with this man? But the truth is, it had never been right between us. He was such a narcissist that nothing could have ever grown between us. Every time I tried to talk to him or reach out to him, he immediately shut me down—and not in any kind or gentle way either. Quite often I would hit the floor after his violence and mental torture. And here I was again, questioning where it had all gone so wrong. And I was fucking angry.

It was time to just give myself space. This was not a time to hurry anything. I was navigating a path that was not society's version of how to respond to the death of a parent. But I couldn't fake how I felt. I'd spent most of the past week feeling nothing at all, but today I was angry. And this was perfectly okay.

I had survived this man's abuse my whole life, and I had arrived at a place where that needed to be honoured. I knew I was safe being in this anger. Was this the first time I had let my feelings spew out into the universe? No, not at all. But this time I knew I could do it and be safe—safe in my own power as the woman I had become. And I knew that never again was that going to be negotiable for anyone!

30 December

After the emotional upheavals of the past two weeks, I decided to spend a day just pottering around in my writing room. I was in my own space, and that was a really good, grounding place to be.

31 December

I planned to spend New Year's Eve at the beach with friends. I was really excited about this because I wanted to put these last two weeks behind me, and somehow I thought that once the clock hit midnight, I could take a deep breath and start fresh. It is odd how that mental perception can happen when a new year begins. But for now, I was just moving along—feeling tired but peaceful—and I just wanted to have some wine and enjoy the night.

1 January 2019

Happy New Year!

I felt that 2019 was going to be a good year and I would just let the year take me where it needed me to be.

I started the year back in my own space, just where I wanted to be. I love my own space. That's where I cope best, where I always feel calm in my spirit. For some, that may not feel right, but we each have to honour what feels right for ourselves, no matter if people are with us or against us. That's all that God ever asks of us. It's not our job to fix everything that's broken in this world. God didn't give us that job. You simply have to honour *you*.

And after everything I'd been through, I was finally ready to honour myself. I was finally ready to give myself what I needed. I was ready to turn the page. I was ready for a new beginning.

And that's exactly what I got.

The Beginning and the End

MY FIRST MEMORY was of taking scissors, trying to cut my sister's hair with them, and being yelled at by my father. Little did I know then that this was just the beginning. As I soon found out, my father would yell at me every day of my childhood, which drove a world of fear into my spirit.

Aside from yelling at me, my father never paid attention to me or took an interest in anything I did. I couldn't lean on him for comfort, go to him for support, or even just spend calm, happy moments in each other's company. And I could never relax around him. He was like a constantly ticking time bomb that could go off at any moment—and frequently did.

Fortunately, though, my father's angry outbursts didn't mar every part of my childhood. I did find some respite in my private world and also in the company of my mother and, even more so, my maternal grandmother.

My mother was a peacemaker—an incredibly strong woman who was very calm in her own spirit. However, because she spent so much time working at our family's dairy farm—and later, as a waitress and kitchen

The Beginning and the End

hand at a local restaurant—she was usually very busy providing for us children. She always provided a calming presence when we were together, though, which served as a welcome balance to my father's volatile personality.

Her father died fairly young, passing away on 1 February 1966—just twenty-three days before I was born. From what I've learned about him, though, I've always felt a connection. We even share the same birthday! My grandmother told me that he was a wonderful man. And he hated my father. He wanted nothing to do with him.

Fortunately, his wife, my grandmother Victoria, lived for many years after that and was a big part of my life. She was the peace of my soul, a precious safe haven for me. I used to visit her every opportunity I got.

My favourite times were when I got to stay with her during holidays. For some reason, I don't remember my brothers ever staying with her for holidays. My sister sometimes came, but much of the time, I was the only one with her—no parents, no siblings, just me and Grandma.

Our visits followed a predictable routine, which provided a welcome change from the chaos of my home.

As soon as I'd arrive, I would jump out of the car and run up to her house. As I reached the front door, I'd be engulfed in the smell of her violets and daphnes, which were her pride and joy. These flowers and their lovely aroma seemed to create an exquisite energy that greeted me the moment I arrived and surrounded her entire home in beauty.

Grandma was always at the front door waiting for big hugs, which I was always happy to give her.

I loved everything about her, even her clothes—the long skirts, jumpers, and cardigans—and I was fascinated by the necklace she always wore, which was made of little gold squares that connected to one another. Somehow I thought it made her

The Beginning and the End

wrinkly neck look stunning, which just goes to show that it's not how a person looks that makes them special but the connection and love we share with them.

When I stayed with Grandma, we would have tea each morning at 10:30, a little ritual that I always looked forward to. She had a burgundy kettle with a beautiful whistle, which to this day is still deeply ingrained in my soul. She also had a silver teapot with a thick, black handle that she would pour our tea from. She only drank English tea, always served on fine bone china.

Grandma's cupboard was full of chocolate teddy bear biscuits, which she would put on our saucers before tea. She knew I loved these biscuits, so she would lay out a few extras for me on a yellow, leaf-shaped dish that she kept on the table. I loved to dip the biscuits in the tea. I was never tidy about this, but Grandma never seemed to mind. She would just laugh and joke about it and then pull out her patterned handkerchiefs to clean up.

As we sipped our tea, she would laugh and say that it was just us ladies. And then, whenever I'd make a mess with the biscuits, she would say, "Oh, Wendyanne, can you eat like a lady?" I would shake my head no, which just made her laugh more. She had this amazing laugh that made me feel so safe.

Another daily ritual that I always looked forward to was the arrival of the mailman, who used to deliver her mail to her door each morning. Sometimes, as he handed her the mail, he would comment on her flowers, which always made her beam with pride.

After the mailman left, I would delight in watching Grandma open each piece of mail with a silver letter opener. When she received handwritten letters from her friends, she would read them aloud to me. I felt a sense that, by sharing these letters, she was sharing joy in the world.

The Beginning and the End

As Grandma saw it, each letter merited a prompt reply. So, as soon as she was done reading, she would pull out her special box that was filled with letters, pens, paper, and stamps, and she would write back to the person who had sent her the letter.

I loved watching her write. Even before I could read, I thought that she had the most exquisite handwriting and that she wrote with such grace.

Posting a letter would never wait, and this became one of our rituals as well. As soon as she finished writing, she would ring for a taxi on an old box phone. While we were waiting, we would put on our hats and coats. My grandmother added to her outfit the most exquisite gloves. She was a real beauty.

Soon, the taxi would arrive, and down the street we would go. I would sit in the back seat with her. I used to watch her hold her handbag with her gloves right in the centre, where the bag would open and close. It was like she was ready to pay the taxi driver at a moment's notice. Even if we still had a way to go, she was already prepared.

When we arrived at the post office, we would get out of the taxi, and then the real gift would begin: she always gave me the duty of posting her letters. I felt like the queen! I finally felt a sense that someone trusted me and gave me a responsibility—the important job of posting her words back to her friends. I felt quite special.

After I'd posted the letter, she would hold my hand as we walked down the street until the taxi would pick us up again.

One day I asked her if she would start writing me letters too. She said she would love that and would always start them with "Dear Wendyanne." For years after that, whenever we weren't together, she often wrote me letters. Each time a new one arrived, I couldn't wait to open it and get my mother to read it to me. In response, I would draw her pictures and send them back to her.

The Beginning and the End

I still have the letters she wrote me, which I will treasure forever.

As much as I loved being with my grandmother at the time, it wouldn't be until years later that I would fully appreciate the moments we shared together. I now realise that she was giving me more than precious memories. She provided a safe haven during a violent time in my life. She provided a calm routine that helped to ground me during a time of chaos and turbulence. She paid attention to me during a time when I was often neglected. She took me seriously and gave me an important responsibility, boosting my sense of self-worth at a time when no one else seemed to trust me or value me. And most of all, she gave me love when I needed it most.

Looking back, I can see that my times with her were soul jewels, gifts that she joyfully shared with me, nourishing me at the deepest level—beautiful memories that I will always hold dear.

When I reflect upon the impact my grandmother had on me, I can see how she inspired the strength that's still within me to this day. When I think of my childhood, times with her are always among the first (and certainly the happiest) memories that pop into my mind—such a beautiful, graceful, loving woman who I still feel walking beside me in spirit every day, especially when I'm writing.

In addition to the time I spent with my grandmother, I enjoyed playing with my sister. I also had a horse called Stardust, who I spent a lot of time with. Aside from that, though, I was pretty much a loner as a child.

Back then, my mother spent most of her time working on the farm, and my father was

The Beginning and the End

usually gone at his job—working on the Country Roads Board, building roads—and when he was home, he was usually yelling, throwing things around the house, or acting abusive in some way, so I quickly learned to keep my distance from him as best as I could.

I also had almost nothing to do with my two brothers. They were older, and from a very young age, my father put them to work on the farm, where they seemed to spend almost all their time.

So, with my other family members out of the house so much, I spent most of my days alone or with my sister, who is three years younger—a significant difference at that age. Perhaps because of this, I was slow to develop in many ways. I could hardly speak until I was five years old, and even then I had trouble forming words. At the time, I was so fearful that I had already closed down. I felt lost in a world that I couldn't understand or connect with.

But even before I could speak, I loved pictures in books and always found comfort in them. From as far back as I can remember, I always wanted to grow up and write books. When I was a young child, my mum would buy me pencils and paper, and I used to make my own books with sticky tape and lots of colours. I had a special little table and chair in my bedroom where I would do my colouring and drawing and create my books.

I felt very peaceful in this world of my imagination, a refuge from my father's world of anger, which I couldn't grasp or even begin to try to understand. I never saw joy in my father's heart, and that was very confusing to me. I think my love for drawing, writing, and creating was a strong foundation I set up in my soul from a very early age as my way to cope.

The Beginning and the End

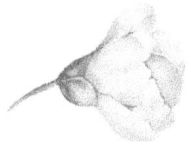

When I started school, I still wasn't speaking much at all, but I enjoyed going to the library to look at the books. While there, I got to know the librarian, Mrs. Tatterson. She was tall and thin and had short brown, curly hair, and she reminded me of my grandmother. She used to wear skirts like Grandma's, as well as jumpers and cardigans, and she always wore pearls. I took to her like a duck takes to water.

I would go to the library every opportunity I got, especially at lunchtime. I couldn't seem to get there quickly enough; I was so excited to look at the books and to see Mrs. Tatterson. She knew I had trouble speaking, and she offered to read me any book I wanted. I would always pick out a book about five little ducklings walking over a hill. We would bring it to the library's old red couch where she would sit with me, reading the story, pointing out the pictures, and asking me questions.

She went about it very gently. I can see now that she wanted to build a connection with me, and it worked. I really trusted her, not just because she read to me and reminded me of my grandmother, but because she was so gentle and patient.

After we'd spent some time together, she would sit with me and spell out words from the book. Then she began to ask me to repeat the words she would say. This went on for a long time. Eventually, she managed to pull some words out of me. I was speaking!

Looking back, I know that Mrs. Tatterson recognized my potential—she saw something in me. Thanks to her patience and gentle encouragement, I grew stronger with my words, and a whole world opened up to me.

Even after I was able to speak, books remained my preferred form of

The Beginning and the End

communication with the world. In books, I found a world I could relate to, which I valued all the more when I was at home because I couldn't relate to my father at all. He was never there for me in any positive way. He seemed to spend his entire life being angry, violent, and abusive. So oftentimes, books really were the only safe place for me.

As I grew older, though, it was harder and harder to stay safe. More and more often, there was no escaping my father's temper, especially when it erupted into violent outbursts.

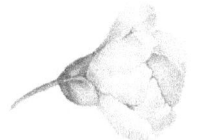

When we were kids, we would celebrate Guy Fawkes Night by lighting off firecrackers. Usually, it was a rare moment of joy for me and my family. But one year, my brother lit a firecracker while my parents were inside. The firecracker didn't go off, though, so my brother went to look at it—to see why it hadn't exploded—when all of sudden it went off and hit him in the eye. My brother started screaming in pain, and I ran inside to tell Dad what had happened.

As he rushed out to my brother, my father pulled my hair and yelled at me, "What in the fuck have you done to your brother?!" He wouldn't let go, and I found myself being dragged along the ground by his hand gripped to the back of my hair. Finally, he dropped me to the ground by an electricity pole, and the back of my head hit the pole, leaving my head sore and the back of my neck bruised from his fingerprints.

That night my brother was taken to Melbourne, where he spent the next six weeks in hospital with my mother beside him. My other brother stayed on the farm, but my sister and I were taken to my cousin Alison's, where

The Beginning and the End

we stayed for the next couple of weeks. Thankfully, my brother did get better, but my father always blamed me for what happened.

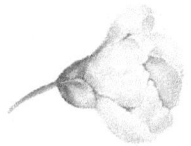

Looking back, I don't think I ever knew what it was like just to be a kid, to be free in the innocence of my own existence, feeling loved by my family and safe in our house. Every day I woke up afraid, not knowing what the day would bring. And all too often, it would bring anger and violent outbursts.

For years I'd been dealing with my father's anger on a daily basis, but by the time I hit my teenage years, his abuse was in full swing. I think it always had been; I was just much more aware of it now. Did I understand it? No, not at all. And I still don't. A narcissistic, abusive parent does not come with instructions.

So I did what I thought was best: I tried to stay as far away from my father as I could. Instead, I continued to focus on books as well as netball, which I loved, and my schooling. I especially loved English and playing the piano. I found myself in all these things, and they brought some much-appreciated comfort into my life. But they still couldn't provide enough of a refuge from my father to keep me safe.

One night I was excited about an upcoming piano recital, and I went out to practice in the shed where my piano was. Shortly after I began practicing, my father burst into the shed in a fit a rage because I hadn't started dinner. Once again, he pulled me by my hair and dragged me into the kitchen and yelled at me to start dinner.

I cooked dinner, and when my mother came in from the farm, she dished out the food. That's when I noticed that there was a chair missing from the table. My father told me to get off my chair and give it to my mother. I was really scared of my father, so usually I didn't dare speak up to him. But this night I'd had enough. I said, "No. *You* get off your chair and give it to Mum." He stood up, and I knew what was coming. He ripped the chair away from me, and I hit the floor so hard that I thought he'd broken my lower back. It hurt for months after that.

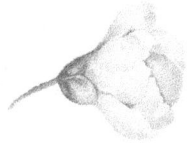

Because my father was always at me about starting dinner—and I knew the consequences if I didn't—I was careful to do all the cooking when Mum wasn't around. One night—while my mum was in hospital to have surgery—I walked into the kitchen and saw that my father had taken a roast out of the freezer, so I put it in the oven to make sure it was cooked in time for dinner. A little while later, though, when he came into the kitchen and saw that I had put the roast in the oven, he started yelling at me at the top of his lungs, saying that the roast was for the weekend. Then he picked up a tea towel, opened the oven door, and threw the whole tray at me—roast and all.

I just couldn't win.

That night, he and I drove in to see Mum. On the ride there, I wanted to keep the peace, so I didn't say a word to him. I just wanted to go see Mum and know that she was going to be okay.

Fortunately, Mum was recovering well from surgery, and we had what I thought was a pleasant visit at the hospital with her. On the way home, though, my father was clearly in a bad mood. He started arguing with me and telling me that I needed to step up because of Mum's surgery. I told him I also had school studies.

The Beginning and the End

Clearly, this was not the reply he was looking for.

He stopped the car on the side of a road and told me to get out of the car and walk home. Mind you, it was 10 p.m. and we were nearly 20 kilometres from home. Without saying a word, I got out in the pitch-black night, and then he drove off.

After a while, he turned around to pick me up. But by this point, the damage was done. I hated the bastard.

I got back into the car and said nothing.

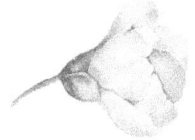

I certainly wasn't the only one who was victimized by my father. My mother frequently endured his temper, as did my siblings. Any infraction, no matter how mild, seemed cause for my father's outbursts. Sometimes his violent attacks were triggered simply because someone was in the wrong place at the wrong time—namely, in my father's way when he was angry.

Which was most of the time.

My sister did her best to stay out of Dad's way. When he came around, she would hide in the wardrobe or on the roof of the shed because she didn't want him to see her. My eldest brother and I tried our best to avoid him too, but sometimes it simply wasn't possible.

I remember one time my father asked my eldest brother to do something. My brother said he couldn't do it just then because he had homework to do. The next thing I knew, he was on the ground and I was watching my father kicking him. I can still see my father's heavy boots striking this young boy, over and over, as he lay helpless on the ground.

On the inside, I was screaming for my father to stop. But so much fear had been

The Beginning and the End

ingrained in me at such a young age, so I didn't dare say anything or lift a finger to help. I knew what would happen if I even tried: I'd be punished even worse, and so would my brother.

Even supposedly happy occasions were marred by my father's mean-spirited behaviour. One time when we were on holiday with friends in Queensland, my father picked my second-eldest brother up by his shorts and top, threw him into the river, and said, "Swim, you bastard!"

Several adults saw this happen, yet no one said anything to my father or did anything to help my brother—a young boy who couldn't swim, fighting for his life with no assurance that he would make it out of the river. He struggled and eventually managed to make his way back to the shore. But at the time, I didn't know—none of us knew—whether or not he would drown right there before our eyes. Yet instead of helping his own son, my father just stood there and laughed—a horrible, maniacal laugh that is still ingrained in me.

Not even the animals were safe from my father's wrath. Shortly after we got back from the holiday in Queensland, my sister got a puppy. Around that time, my grandmother was visiting us on the farm. One night, while she and my sister were picking vegetables for dinner, the puppy got in the way of one of my father's rages. He pulled out his gun and shot the puppy dead—right in front of my grandmother and my sister.

Unfortunately, this wasn't the only time he killed our family pets. He frequently shot our dogs. And one time he shot my guinea pig for no reason at all—other than that it was small, helpless, and an easy target.

I wish I could have spoken up during these times. Where was my voice? Why could I not use it?

The Beginning and the End

It had taken me years to learn to speak, finally willing myself to do it—letter by letter, sound by sound, word by word—but for all the good my voice was doing me now, I may as well have been mute after all. I wasn't able to speak up to defend my mother, my siblings, my pets, or myself. And when I did speak up, it always seemed to backfire, causing even more trouble and abuse.

But that didn't mean I wasn't angry—and growing more angry each day, with each new outrage I had to witness or endure. The rage that was building within me was like a volcano ready to erupt, and all I could hope was that my father would fall into it.

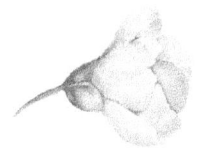

Looking back, I see the impossible position I was put in. I was just a child; I was powerless to stop him. But what about the adults? What about the people who *could* have spoken up? They could have done something, stood up to my father, stopped the abuse, said *Enough!*

Today, if my father did what he did back then—the domestic abuse and animal abuse—he would be in jail. Yet back then, he faced no consequences whatsoever.

Even though no one pressed criminal charges, they still could have stepped in to help us—or, at the very least, reprimand my father for his despicable cruelty.

Yet they were silent.

At the time, I couldn't fathom why no one defended us children, and I still can't wrap my head around it. In most cases, I think it's because my father pulled the wool over people's eyes. He was such a charmer when people came to our home, but once they'd leave he would turn into a monster. But even

The Beginning and the End

when they did witness his abuse, they never spoke up—such as the friends who saw him throw my brother into the river. Even then, as a child, I wondered, How could these people just watch? Why did no one step in to help while it was happening—or, at the very least, rebuke my father afterwards?

It amazes me that this brother—the one I'm now estranged from—somehow kept his bond with my father even after years of mistreatment. Maybe he had a longer fuse, but mine had run out. After meekly putting up with my father's abuse throughout my childhood, I'd finally had enough. I now hated this man.

As the anger and abuse at home escalated, I threw myself more and more into my schoolwork, finding solace and escape in a world of reading, writing, and learning. And the more I focused on these areas, the more I excelled in them. Soon, my year 9 English teacher, Miss Bolton, began to take notice. One day she pulled me aside and told me I was very gifted in my writing. "You should write and never stop," she said. I smiled at her, but it wouldn't be until years later that I would fully understand her advice.

Unfortunately, my positive achievements at school led to negative consequences at home. My father read my school report that year—one of the only ones he ever bothered to look at—and saw that I'd gotten an A+ in English and typing as well as an award for excellence. He just sneered and said, in a voice dripping with sarcasm, "I'm glad you can spell and type." My blood began to boil. I felt sick just being around this man. Little did I know

The Beginning and the End

that this moment would lead to something far more sickening.

My mother used to run our family's dairy farm, and she also got a job at night in a restaurant, so we kids were often left alone with our father. One night he called me into the kitchen. I immediately sensed that something unusual was going on—for the first time I could remember, the typewriter was sitting on the kitchen table. My father fixed me with a strange look. "I see you can spell, and you can type also," he said.

I nodded. I didn't know what he was leading to, but I had an ominous feeling that it wouldn't be pleasant.

It wasn't.

He explained that he wanted me to type a letter to a young woman he had recently met and started seeing. He recited, and word by word, I typed everything he told me to. The letter was extremely explicit. I wanted to rip it out of the typewriter and choke him with the paper. But I didn't dare back answer or question him because I knew what the consequences would be—his black leather belt was right beside him on the chair. So I did what I had to do: I typed the letter and then left without a word.

I was thirteen years old.

Over the next few months, these letter-writing sessions became regular occurrences. Each time I'd see the typewriter on the table, I'd feel sick to my guts. I wanted it all to stop, but I was too scared to stand up to my father or to say anything to my mother. If my father found out I'd told her, he would have flown into one of his rages. But Mum did find out about the affair. It wasn't difficult for her to discover: my father and his girlfriend weren't exactly discreet about it. She replied to his letters, sending them directly to our family home, and my mum knew all about it because my brother used to steam them open.

The Beginning and the End

Each time a new letter arrived, I knew I'd have to sit with my father and type up his lurid reply with him sitting beside me while my mother was off at work. I felt trapped, helpless. I couldn't see a way out. I knew what would happen if I refused. His black leather belt was always within arm's reach on the table.

And so I typed.

My love of writing was now poisoned. I began hating English class. I rebelled more and more, and I no longer even tried to get good marks. I just gave up. Miss Bolton noticed and expressed her concern, but I never told her what had caused my change.

It was also around this time that I developed a new coping mechanism—one that would almost claim my life.

Robbed of the comfort I'd once found in books and school, I no longer had a way to release my anxiety. I went through each day feeling scared, nervous, and sick to my stomach. Eventually, though, I did find a way to release my anxiety—by vomiting my guts out.

More and more, I found comfort in this. It was a way for me to purge and scream and let out some of the toxic energy I'd been carrying around. And, if only for a few minutes, I felt good. But then one day I began to vomit blood.

My mother took me to a doctor, and after undergoing several tests, I learned that I had ripped the lining of my stomach and was now bleeding internally. I also learned that I had a condition called bulimia nervosa. And I

The Beginning and the End

learned that I was in even worse shape than I had realised.

For the first of many times in the coming years, I had to be hospitalised.

At this stage, I was in a very bad way—physically, mentally, and emotionally. I was still suffering from severe anxiety, and I had no way to release it aside from vomiting. So for much of my time in the hospital, I was kept under heavy sedation. Even in that state, though, I knew that my life was a mess, and I secretly wanted God to take me home.

Despite my horrible condition, my times of being hospitalised did offer one huge advantage: at least I was away from my father. For the first time in years, I felt safe.

This time also marked a huge turning point in my family's life: my parents got divorced.

After my parents split up, I had nothing to do with my father for a few years. I spent those years finishing secondary school and, with a lot of medical assistance, recovering from my eating disorder. Shortly thereafter, I met a man I felt safe with, and when I was twenty-one, we got married.

In retrospect, I realise that it was a mistake for me to get married then. I was too young and unstable, and I was mainly doing it because I just wanted to feel safe. Another mistake was that I asked my father to come to the wedding, which opened the door to let him back into my life, which I never should have done.

The best part of being married is that I had two beautiful children, who I love with all my heart. Not surprisingly, though, the marriage didn't last, and something began to rumble within me.

The Beginning and the End

The next chapter of my life was an unravelling—I was unbecoming everything I was not and becoming everything I was meant to be. I started therapy to explore what was happening to me—to unpack what I'd been through and learn how to move forward in healthy ways. But I didn't know that at the time. I just knew I needed help.

During my first session, my therapist asked me, "What has brought you here today?" I told her I didn't know, and she said, "Okay then. How about we start at the start." So we did, and for the next fifteen years, we unravelled it all, stitch by stitch.

As time went on and I progressed in my therapy, I wanted to rediscover if I could have a relationship with my father. I was now a mum, and I worried about letting him back into my life—for my children's sake as well as my own. Yet I wanted to give it one more chance.

So, one morning I went to a coffee shop and wrote him a letter saying that I wanted to meet with him and build something with him. I told him that I wanted my father in my life, and I wanted my children to have a grandfather.

But he never replied.

A few years later, I went back to the same coffee shop and wrote him another letter asking if we could meet—to talk, reconnect, and try to build our relationship. But, like the first one, this letter went unacknowledged.

And yet I persisted. I kept reaching out to him. In retrospect, this was a big mistake—not because we weren't able to reconnect but because, eventually, we did. And in many ways, we picked up right where we'd left off.

Because I was an adult, he could no longer push me around as he'd done when I was a child, but his venom was as potent as ever. For the next few years, his verbal and emotional toxicity became a regular part of my life once again. Still, no matter how much he berated, belittled, and disrespected me, I held out hope that things could improve between us, that somehow he'd eventually become the kind, loving father I'd always wanted but never had.

As I continued therapy, however, I started to figure out that the relationship with my father was never going to be based on healthy positivity and nourishment; it would always be based on his narcissism and cruelty. I would always be undermining myself while he was in my life.

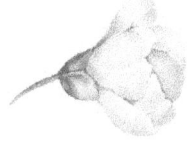

Fortunately, the years following my divorce were also filled with positive developments in my life. Being a single mum was difficult, but I cherished the time with my babies. During this time, I also felt a desire to reconnect with my writing, so I enrolled in the Australian College of Journalism in Sydney and began a diploma program in writing. Through this program, I found the connection back to Miss Bolton's encouraging words to me in year 9. Writing was now at the forefront of my life and would play an even bigger role in what was about to unfold.

After graduating, I had another baby and took some time off to focus on my own healing. Through therapy, I continued to explore my relationship with my father, and I came to realise that healing emotional trauma and trying to raise emotionally healthy children is powerful, powerful work for this planet. It was also very painful at times, but I knew I had to keep going.

My father still had such a hold on me, but I was slowly breaking free from his chains. First, though, I had to reach my own breaking point.

The Beginning and the End

When I was pregnant with my last baby, my father came to visit me at my home unannounced; he just showed up with his new partner and casually said that he'd just been to see one of his friends—a man who used to come camping on our farm with his wife and family, a man who'd had no boundaries with me, a man who had molested me when I was twelve years old. To make matters even worse, my father had known what was happening and had done nothing—not one thing to stop him, not one thing to defend the daughter he was supposed to protect. And now, he was still friends with this man, discussing his recent visit as casually as he'd mention the weather—as if there were no problem at all, as if nothing had ever happened, as if, through his silence and inaction, he hadn't been a knowing accomplice in this abuse.

In that moment, something in me snapped. After all the years of horrific abuse I'd suffered at my father's hands, this was the last straw. Enough was enough.

I asked him to leave, and then I somehow found the courage to go to the police station and talk to a police woman about my father's friend. I told her about what had happened, and she said my father would have to make a statement. But I knew he wouldn't support me, so there seemed to be no other options for legal action. On a personal level, though, I knew what I had to do.

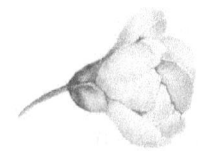

The Beginning and the End

I decided to completely break away from this dysfunctional relationship with my father that had fucked up my life for far too long. I wasn't going to let it happen for one more day. This relationship was no longer going to steal any more oxygen from my life. It had to be dismantled. It had to end.

I continued my therapy and got stronger. I worked on my boundary muscle, my self-expression muscle, my self-care muscle, and my sanity muscle. And I removed my father from my life.

I believe we all have a turning point—a point of no going back—and I had finally reached this point. Things had forever changed, realigned. But, as I realised, true alignment doesn't require you to change who you are; it requires you to *be* who you are. And for the first time ever, I was learning to be myself. I was coming home to myself.

For the next eight years, I didn't see my father. During this time, I focused on being the best mum I could be, I bought a home, and I kept working on myself in therapy and on my own. I had come a long way from the meek little girl who was too afraid to stand up to her father, but I still hadn't rid myself of his influence over me, not by a long shot. I knew I had to make a shift that was bigger than anything I had done before, so I prayed to God and I never stopped praying.

A week later, my prayers were answered—but not in the way I would have expected. Nearly a decade after his last visit, my father once again showed up unannounced at my home.

I answered the door and immediately felt sick. But in that moment, my boundary weakened. I said hello and asked him in for a cup of tea. Fortunately, he declined. He said he was just in the neighbourhood. But he wouldn't come in. I'm glad he didn't.

My youngest daughter came skipping down the hallway and asked who was there. I told her not to worry about it, that I had it handled. After she left, I told my father, "If she comes back, you are not to tell her who you are. She doesn't know you."

We talked for five minutes, and then he left. That was the last time I ever saw him.

My father showing up that day turned out to be just what I needed. I probably shouldn't have opened the door in the first place, but I'm actually glad I did because his visit helped me reach the next level of clarity. It helped me see the light—and to rediscover my own light. It helped me reclaim my power and embrace my inner warrior. It helped me see that it was time to make a decisive break. I just couldn't go through this again.

Three days after his last visit, once I'd rebalanced myself, I went to my favourite coffee shop—the same one where I'd gone to write the previous two letters to him, the same one where I would later go to process his death on the morning after he passed away—and over the next four mornings, I sat there and wrote him a letter that no daughter should ever have to write to her father. I never wanted to have to write him a letter like this, but it was long overdue.

In this letter, I finally expressed my outrage for all the years of abuse.
For all the times he had neglected me.

The Beginning and the End

For all the times he had failed to protect me.

For all the times he had yelled at me.

For all the times he had threatened me.

For all the times he had hit me.

For all the times he had dragged me by my hair.

For all the times he abused my mother, my brothers, and my sister.

For all the times he had killed my pets.

For all the times he had hurt me.

For all the times he had made me type dirty letters to his mistress.

For the childhood he had robbed me of.

For the little girl who would never have the daddy she deserved.

But this letter was not coming from a girl with hopes of building a relationship with her father. It was coming from a powerful woman who had found her strength. A woman who had found her strong boundaries, her self-worth, her self-respect, her voice, her life. It was long overdue.

As I wrote, I felt the truth of those words of Miss Bolton, my year 9 English teacher, all those years ago when she told me how powerful my writing was. On this day, writing that letter in the coffee shop, I felt that power and I focused it into every word I wrote.

At this point, I had accepted one hundred percent that this man could no longer be anywhere near me, and I made it abundantly clear that if he ever again attempted to make contact with me, I would have an intervention order taken out on him in a heartbeat.

I wrote the letter for legal reasons—so that I had it in writing that he was never to contact me again. I wrote it for him—so that he would have to confront the consequences of his abuse. But above all else, I wrote it for myself.

This letter was a defining moment for me and my relationship with my father, and it was also a defining moment for me and my life. It was my declaration of independence, my emancipation, my way of claiming my power and asserting my strength.

It was my way of saying, at long last, *Enough!*

After four days of pouring my heart, my soul, my rage, and my power onto the page, I finished the letter and posted it to him. And I got my wish: I never heard from him again. It had taken forty-five years, but he was finally out of my life for good.

A Fresh Start

A COUPLE OF WEEKS after my father's funeral, I went to visit my sister. It was so spontaneous, as we had been estranged from each other for some time now. But for some reason, something was telling me to go and visit her today.

My sister had not been particularly close to our father either, but she did have communication with him and had been with him from the time of his brain haemorrhage until his passing.

I arrived at her home not knowing how I would be greeted, but we were both daughters of this man—and we were still sisters, after all—so I thought I would just let go and let God take this day where it needed to go.

I knocked on the door, and my sister answered and invited me in. I went inside, and we immediately hugged. It felt so right.

It turned out to be a beautiful day. We had a cup of tea by the pool, and the conversation flowed easily and naturally. She said she was going up to Dad's house, and I asked if she wanted company. She said yes.

I had not been to his home for fifteen years, so I felt very uncomfortable just thinking about going back there. But I had decided to let this day with my sister take us where it needed to go. So, off we went.

A Fresh Start

We drove up and stayed at his home for a while, just looking around the house and walking in the garden. I asked her if she wanted to go and visit his grave, and she said yes. So, again, off we went.

I told her that I had come to his grave the night of his funeral. But this time, instead of leaving after two minutes, we stayed for an hour.

We went to our father's grave first. After that, we spent the rest of the hour looking around at all the graves in the cemetery, fixing the flowers that had blown off them.

It was really nice to just spend time with my sister, and for the first time in a very long time, I felt a connection with her.

After leaving the cemetery, we went into town and bought lunch and took it to the park. As we sat together at a picnic table, eating and talking, she told me about the morning of our father's brain haemorrhage and how it had been four hours before an ambulance was called. She described how he was in hospital and told me that his partner had asked her, "When is Wendyanne coming?"

"She isn't," my sister had said.

She then continued describing the last days and hours up until his passing. She looked at me across the table and said, "Wendy, it was just bloody awful. It was just the saddest thing I've ever seen." And then she started crying.

I had no idea what to say. I simply wasn't feeling like she was.

We were sisters who should have been going through this the same way, but we were coming into this passing from two completely different angles. We both needed comforting, and neither one of us knew how to fully provide it.

But I was listening, and we were talking, and that was a great place to start.

Forgiveness Through Different Eyes

FORGIVENESS.
I cannot tell you how many times I've negotiated with this word. Again and again, I've tried to wrap my head around it, untangle it, comprehend it. I've dissected it. Wrestled

with it. Bashed myself up with it. Sent myself into a downward spiral trying to fathom this elusive, multifaceted, complex, and seemingly impenetrable word.

Forgiveness.

In my quest to get to the bottom of this word—and access its power—I searched through every book I could get my hands on that I thought might give me some kind of clarity about this word and why it had such a tight grip on me.

Over and over, I heard that if I wanted to heal—to truly be free—I needed to forgive my father. But there was just one problem: I didn't *want* to forgive him. I hated this man and everything he had done. I thought that if I forgave him, I would be saying that what he did was okay. And it most certainty was *not* okay. None of it was.

When I sat in that coffee shop for four consecutive mornings and wrote him that final letter, I clarified something within my body, mind, and soul: I was finally taking back my power. I was finally showing up for myself. I felt strong, solid, and firm in my commitment to live my best life, free from this man's tyranny and abuse.

And for the rest of his life, my commitment never wavered.

After his death, I thought I was done with this whole issue of forgiveness. But over the years, I've found that it can be persistent.

As my emotional healing progressed and I continued to explore the impact of the relationship with my father—on my own, through therapy, and while writing this book—the idea of forgiveness kept returning, over and over. And gradually, my understanding and experience of forgiveness evolved.

Forgiveness means something different to everyone, as every individual's experience is unique to them. To me, it used to mean condoning someone's behaviour—letting them off the hook—which I certainly did not want to do. But as I emerged from a period of metamorphosis following my father's death, I reached a new understanding of this word—something that I could live with, something that allowed me to feel at peace with myself and with my past. After much reflection, this is what forgiveness now means to me in relation to this journey with my father:

First and foremost, by opening myself to forgiveness of any kind, I am *not* condoning what he did. I am not saying that it was right, good, or okay on any level. It is—and always was—absolutely unacceptable. The way he treated me—and others—was cruel, malicious, and downright mean. Nobody should ever be subjected to such disrespect, mistreatment, and abuse. Period.

I still wholeheartedly feel this way about what he did. However, I eventually came to realise that if I was going to hold on to this anger, resentment, and pain, I would never be free. I would never be able to unbecome the person I did not want to be and grow into my higher potential, the woman I am meant to be.

So, as much as I didn't want to revisit those dark times from my past, I felt that this was a critical part of my inner work. I had to feel every single emotion to get through to the other side.

One of the first steps of this process was to forgive myself—to let go of guilt and shame surrounding what happened with my father, to let go of the belief that somehow I was responsible for any of it. Because I wasn't.

In addition to reflecting on my childhood, I began to focus more and more on loving and respecting myself *now*—moving beyond old, unhealthy patterns and becoming a strong adult, a mature woman who does not negotiate her power for anyone. And this is who I have grown into.

But perhaps above all else for me, forgiveness has come to mean *freedom*. I did not want to be mentally or emotionally chained to this man anymore, so I was willing to do the difficult inner work to heal from him—to free myself from him. And once I did, I truly was free in every way. I could be happily present in my life. And, as I've discovered, this is a great place to be.

One of the surprising gifts to come from this entire experience—living through and healing from my past, including my father's death—is gratitude.

Forgiveness Through Different Eyes

Until fairly recently, I never would have believed this possible, but I can now say that I am actually grateful for many of the gifts in my life because of my father.

For one thing, my father taught me a lot about what I do *not* want in this world: violence, anger, mean-spirited bullying, and basically everything he embodied. So I now gravitate towards the opposite of this: kindness, calmness, goodness, and peace.

After so many years of watching my father's cruelty, I chose a life of compassion and empathy for those who are suffering—especially animals and young children. For instance, when I see an insect in my path, I carefully step over or around it. When I see a butterfly trapped in a hedge, I gently set it free. And when I find out that one of my kindergarten students is having a hard time at home, I make a point of giving them extra attention and responsibility—anything to help them feel special and know that they are seen, valued, and loved.

Living with my father taught me to be fearful, but it also made me patient and resilient. I had to be, or I wouldn't have kept getting back up after being knocked down so many times!

It also taught me to appreciate the basic freedoms that so many people take for granted. After feeling trapped for so many years—unable to break away from him physically or emotionally—I cherish the feeling of freedom I have now that he is no longer here. Feeling free is one of the most powerful energies we can ever hold in our own spirit, and it is something I will never take for granted again.

Over the years, I've learned to follow the light, but not because my father embodied light—in fact, it was just the opposite: he saw only darkness and brought darkness wherever he went. But I knew from a young age that I never wanted to be anything like him. I didn't want to see the world the way he did. So I didn't. I saw the light in the world. That was my path to discover, and I did.

Despite everything I've endured, I never saw myself as a victim, partly because all the emotional hardships, negative experiences, and abuse I suffered at my father's hand have taught me to appreciate all the small steps I have taken—and continue to take—towards my healing. They also taught me to appreciate all the small, positive steps I see others taking in their own lives. No matter how small these steps may seem from the outside, I see each one as significant, as I believe that our greatest strength is not in one ultimate victory but in the hundreds of little victories we add to our lives as we heal.

Above all, my journey with my father has taught me to appreciate all the blessings of this world that surround me each and every day. I now see miracles in the simplest of things: a sunrise, a sunset, a flower, sitting in peace, laughing with children and friends, butterflies, the ocean, good food, hugs, gentleness, reconnecting with my writing, watching the steam rise from a hot cup of tea—all those things you don't notice when you're stuck in survival mode.

After years of not caring whether I lived or died, I now feel blessed for each and every day of life.

So, did I ever forgive my father? Well, I genuinely hope he is at peace. But the way I see it, it was never my job to forgive him; it was my job to understand that I could set myself free from him…and then to do it.

And that is the journey I continue to this day—the journey towards ever-expanding freedom, the journey towards myself.

It has been a long journey of coming home to myself after removing my father from my life, but he truly is out of my life now. Aside from thinking about him while writing this book, he rarely crosses my mind. He plays almost no role in my present life, and I suspect that his hold on me will diminish even further now that I'm nearly done writing this book. I'm already feeling a sense of closure, a sense of freedom, a sense of peace.

Yes, I still have some triggers, but their power over me decreases each day. I've even managed to let go of a lot of the anger I used to feel regarding his cruelty towards me and others, as I've learned to accept what I can't change—including everything that happened in the past. I now know that this dark past doesn't have to doom me to a dark future.

The bulb of the flower always starts in the dirt. I too feel like my life began in a deep, dark place, full of dirt, devoid of light. But now I feel like I'm finally ready to release that dark past, emerge into the light, and bloom. And every day, I consciously open up more and more towards the light, embracing the many blessings and joys of this life.

The peace I now feel within my own body, mind, and soul is truly beautiful, and I will continue to add more things to my own life that nourish me. I will keep creating peaceful relationships, peaceful environments, and peaceful energy around me. And I will nurture these beautiful people, things, and experiences. I will cherish them.

Many people's grieving process does follow the familiar pattern we've heard about so many times—the pattern that most people have come to expect, including intense sadness and a longing to have the person back. However, I now understand that sometimes we do experience grief through different eyes. For me, this has been one of those times. And that is okay. It is all okay.

I have written this book as part of my own healing process, but I hope it helps others heal as well—perhaps even you. If you're grieving, I hope that reading this has helped you on your journey. I hope it encourages you to follow your own path, to find your own voice, and to use it to honour your precious soul. I hope that it has opened your eyes to different ways to grieve. And I hope that it has further opened your heart—to others and to yourself.

Grieving is a very personal journey. It doesn't always look like the textbook examples. Everyone grieves in their own unique way, and that is perfectly okay. More than okay—it's beautiful.

Epilogue

EVEN THOUGH it's only been three years since my father passed away, it feels like another era. I've gone through so much healing since then and grown so much. In some ways, a lot has changed since his passing. In other ways, my life is very much as it was beforehand.

Following the six-week break after my father passed, I went back into kindergarten and had another beautiful year with the new children. The following year, I took a week off at Christmas and spent it at the beach—finally able to enjoy a true holiday. And now, I'm just living my own life—happy, free, and full of love.

I have very strong faith, and I've made peace with everything that's happened with my father, even his passing. I live my life now fully in gratitude, love, and serenity. I'm at home with myself. There's something very beautiful in the grace I have now in the centre of my soul.

I'm finally in a good place—inside and out. After years of feeling unworthy, my self-worth is solid. I practice self-care and feel self-love. I no longer survive in fear; I now live in love and patience. I enjoy my writing and my work with children.

Epilogue

This doesn't mean that everything is now perfect or easy for me, though. I'm still estranged from one of my brothers, primarily because of my severing my connection with Dad. And while I do talk with my other brother, I wish he lived closer so we could see each other more. However, I have fully reconnected with my sister, and we are now the closest we've ever been. I'm confident that in the coming years, we'll continue to rebuild the bond that weakened due in part to my father.

I also have a loving relationship with my mum, even though it can be difficult for her when I discuss this book or the fact that I'm revisiting the past, which she would rather not dwell on.

It's also challenging for her because I've changed so much during the course of writing this book, going through therapy, and processing everything I've gone through. It almost feels like we have to create a whole new relationship based on the person I've become.

I do admire her for surviving what she went through and for getting out of that toxic marriage. I realise that in those days, women didn't have the support that they do now, so it must have taken tremendous strength and courage for her to break away—something that I am forever grateful to her for doing.

I simply have to accept that her healing process is different from my own. She seems to be content now just being able to put the kettle on in peace. To her, that is heaven.

So, my father is gone, out of my life, departed from this world. Do I grieve for him?

Epilogue

No. I already did that while he was still alive. I am done with grieving for him.

And do I miss him? Not at all. I'm relieved, glad he's nowhere near my life anymore. Now that he's gone, I feel as light, peaceful, and free as a butterfly.

All my love,
Wendyanne

Acknowledgements

LIFE WILL BRING YOU THE PEOPLE you need at just the right time. When I began to write this book, God put the most beautiful, strong man into my path—a man named Tony D. Brown. This is the beautiful soul who would gently take my hand and give me the strength that I so needed to keep going.

One day I gave Tony my manuscript to read, and he was kind enough to offer his helpful feedback. He said he thought that I could go deeper with my words. He knew that a lot of the story was missing, and he recommended that I watch a movie called *The Book Thief*, so I did. It was a movie about love, cruelty, strength, war, and the power of literature. This movie reinforced the message that Tony shared with me: I too had the power to go deeper, reconnect with my own story, and not let it go, no matter what came up. "Just keep going, Wendyanne," Tony said to me. "You have the depth to do it. Trust yourself. You can do it."

Thanks to this beautiful, dedicated, loving man, I was able to not only write my story but also share the depths of my soul. Tony, your encouragement and guidance were just what I needed to gain my butterfly wings and fly to freedom. Thank you. I love you with all my heart.

Acknowledgements

This book would not have come together without the most incredible writing coaches and editors, Dan Teck and Jodi Chapman, two beautiful human beings who have guided, taught, and encouraged me through their words of love, strength, and support. Because of Dan and Jodi, I now have a writing family of many beautiful souls who have also listened to me, supported me, and encouraged me through this journey. Through this writing group, God has given me the blessings and love of surrounding me with more earth angels who have helped make this book possible. Thank you to everyone in this lovely, supportive community.

I also want to thank Jay Renalson, the counsellor who has supported me throughout my journey for the past twenty-five years.

When I decided to begin therapy, it was important for me to work with someone I could trust and feel a connection with. Fortunately, I had that instantly with Jay. The very first time I walked into her office, the first words she said to me were, "Hello, Wendyanne. What has brought you here today?"

I said, "I don't know where to start."

"Well then, how about you start at the start," Jay replied in the most loving, gentle voice.

At that time, I was an extremely fragile young woman, reluctant to open up and trust anyone—much less a complete stranger. But something in her voice—and the kind, gentle energy behind her words—let me know that I was in the presence of an earth angel. I was safe.

Very early on in our connection, she saw something in me that needed to come out, and in all the time we've been connected, not once has she faltered in her love, support, and strength as she's guided me into my peace.

For a quarter century, this incredible therapist has seen me sad, angry, confused, and brought to my knees, exhausted from

Acknowledgements

working through this difficult journey of healing from my father's abuse—a journey that no daughter or son should ever have to travel, but one that I'm grateful I didn't have to take alone. Thanks to Jay's patience and dedication, I've been able to work and work and rework my way through my most difficult life experiences—with my father and in other areas—opening up, exploring, grieving, processing, and healing until I untangled myself from my father's abuse, found my voice, found my strength, and found myself.

In addition to wise, compassionate guidance, Jay has given me the tools to ensure that I will never lose myself again. She is an incredible human being, full of patience, gentleness and grace. I am forever grateful for you, Jay.

I am also blessed to have some very special friends who have given me unconditional love and support as I was writing and throughout my life. I consider these beautiful souls to be earth angels:

Janine Minchin, thank you for being one of my best friends from way back in school, for always being only a phone call away, and for sharing your love, as gentle as an angel.

Narelle Petterson, thank you for always checking in. You have always been so encouraging and kept me going in writing this book. Your support means the world to me.

Kylie Johnson Spiller, thank you for being an amazing, beautiful soul who has listened to me, offered unconditional support, and lovingly encouraged me every step of the way.

Tracey Warry, thank you for being like a sister to me and for being one of the most loving human beings I know.

Lee Sellings, thank you for always caring and loving in the beautiful way that you do.

Michael Brewer, thank you for listening to my ideas and guiding me beautifully with my writing. I so value our friendship and your ability to know exactly how to be gentle,

Acknowledgements

loving, supportive, and full of encouragement for me and this book.

Thank you to all of you beautiful earth angels in my world. I love you all.

In Loving Memory

I want to thank my grandmother, Victoria. I feel like the luckiest woman for having her in my life for twenty-three years—receiving her wisdom, benefiting from her grounding energy, and creating the most loving memories, which I keep forever in my heart.

I also want to thank my best friend, Carol, who passed away from cancer on 28 March 2004. Carol and I had the most incredible bond. When we met, so many years ago, we connected immediately, and that connection remained strong right to the end. Carol had such a softness and warmth about her that in her company you couldn't help but feel loved. Her favourite saying was, "Baby girl, we are on the path." Yes, Carol, we are.

Finally, I want to thank my beloved friend Duane. Several years ago, I spoke to him about the possibility of writing a book about my father. Duane encouraged me to pursue this idea and planted the seed that if I did, I would do it well—and all in divine timing. He was such an important part of my life and a huge reason why this book exists at all.

Last year—on 15 March 2021—I received a call that Duane had committed suicide.

My feelings about the two deaths I was now processing—Duane's and my father's—hit me from very different angles. I felt like I had lost and grieved my father years earlier, but navigating Duane's suicide felt very different. He had meant so much to me in life, and I only wish he could have felt the love for himself that I felt for him.

Acknowledgements

I had nowhere to go with any of these feelings except to surrender to faith. Only now, a year and a half after his passing, am I able to feel Duane's spirit around me.

May he rest in peace.

About the Author

WENDYANNE PAKULSKY is passionate about reminding people that with every life shift comes an opportunity for growth and healing into new heights of awareness.

She lives in a lovely small town in the Australian province of Victoria, where she teaches kindergarten and enjoys gardening and spending time with her family and their sausage dogs.

After receiving her diploma from the Australian College of Journalism (Sydney), Wendyanne has written in a variety of genres.

She has contributed to several personal-growth books, including four books in the 365 Book Series—*365 Moments of Grace*, *365 Life Shifts: Pivotal Moments That Changed Everything*, *Goodness Abounds: 365 True Stories of Loving Kindness*, and *365 Soulful Messages: The Right Guidance at the Right Time*—as well as *Soul Biz: Practical Tips & Heartfelt Wisdom for Entrepreneurs, Solopreneurs, & Creative Souls*.

She has also written books for children, including *Miss Pickles*, an illustrated book about a composting worm.

About the Author

Wendyanne is passionate about the importance of reading regularly to children. Her mission is to continue to write for children, to encourage adults to spend quality time with them, and to open children's minds to the world of creative stories that touch their hearts and also teach positive life lessons.

Connect with Wendyanne on Facebook at www.facebook.com/wendy.anne.10.

www.ingramcontent.com/pod-product-compliance
Lightning Source LLC
Chambersburg PA
CBHW071704040426
42446CB00011B/1913